Olive and Hilary

A Play

Geraldine Aron

SAMUELFRENCH-LONDON.CO.UK
SAMUELFRENCH.COM

Copyright © 1996 by Geraldine Aron
All Rights Reserved

OLIVE AND HILARY is fully protected under the copyright laws of the British Commonwealth, including Canada, the United States of America, and all other countries of the Copyright Union. All rights, including professional and amateur stage productions, recitation, lecturing, public reading, motion picture, radio broadcasting, television and the rights of translation into foreign languages are strictly reserved.

ISBN 978-0-573-12186-9

www.samuelfrench-london.co.uk

www.samuelfrench.com

FOR AMATEUR PRODUCTION ENQUIRIES

UNITED KINGDOM AND WORLD EXCLUDING NORTH AMERICA
plays@SamuelFrench-London.co.uk
020 7255 4302/01

Each title is subject to availability from Samuel French,

depending upon country of performance.

CAUTION: Professional and amateur producers are hereby warned that *OLIVE AND HILARY* is subject to a licensing fee. Publication of this play does not imply availability for performance. Both amateurs and professionals considering a production are strongly advised to apply to the appropriate agent before starting rehearsals, advertising, or booking a theatre. A licensing fee must be paid whether the title is presented for charity or gain and whether or not admission is charged.

The professional rights in this play are controlled by Samuel French Ltd, 52 Fitzroy Street, London, W1T 5JR.

No one shall make any changes in this title for the purpose of production. No part of this book may be reproduced, stored in a retrieval system, or transmitted in any form, by any means, now known or yet to be invented, including mechanical, electronic, photocopying, recording, videotaping, or otherwise, without the prior written permission of the publisher. No one shall upload this title, or part of this title, to any social media websites.

The right of Geraldine Aron to be identified as author of this work has been asserted by her in accordance with Section 77 of the Copyright, Designs and Patents Act 1988

CHARACTERS

Olive Early 40s. A sunny, innocent personality. She dresses New Age style in layers of pink, with pink-tinted hair.

Hilary Early 40s. Absurdly happy. Favours purple, including her hair.

Monica Late 30s. Brittle and bossy. Beautifully dressed and groomed.

Ernest Any age. A taxi driver. Good-natured and courteous.

Bernard Middle-aged. Timid. Ginger hair and a fondness for ginger clothes.

NB: Ernest and Bernard can be played by the same actor.

Place: the living-room of a modest house, perhaps outside Dublin, in Ireland.

Time: the present.

**For
Marion Walsh-Riggs
with love**

OLIVE AND HILARY

Scene 1

The living-room of a modest house, perhaps outside Dublin, in Ireland

Hilary and Olive are preparing for the arrival of Olive's sister, Monica. The room reflects their interest in New Age. There are crystals of all shapes and sizes and many mystic images and icons, including angels. The dominating colours of the room are pink and purple. The space is very cluttered. There is a small table and two unmatched chairs, a rug on the floor, shelves with objects on them, including a telephone concealed with a tea cosy and a cassette player. There is a tall bookcase, on the top shelf of which is a stone jar and a kitchen timer. There is a mirror on one wall, a picture with a price list on the back on another wall and curtains at the window. A large folding screen, decorated with angels, stands folded at the back. A rolled-up futon serves as a sofa. There are exits to the hall and to the kitchen

Olive moves various items around in an attempt to render the room more orderly

Hilary enters with an armful of pink and purple cushions

Hilary These are still a bit damp. Will I group them or scatter them?

Olive takes a break from polishing a large chunk of crystal with the hem of her cotton skirt

Olive I'd say scatter them so they can air.

Hilary stands in the centre of the room, closes her eyes, and scatters the cushions

Hilary (*scattering*) I was reading about an interior decorator in New York who gets paid a thousand dollars to do this.
Olive Go 'way.
Hilary No kidding. When he finishes, they take polaroids so the maids will have a reference. I think it was at your woman Ivana Trump's place.
Olive Will I take a couple of photos then, for when it's my turn to scatter them?

Hilary throws a cushion at her

Well. It looks really beautiful.
Hilary If we say so ourselves. I'll put the lentils on.

Hilary exits

Olive takes a final look around, then sits cross-legged on the floor, her upturned palms on her knees. She closes her eyes and meditates, softly extolling her mantra

Olive Ahh-emmmmm. Ahh-emmmmm. Ahh——

She is interrupted by a cheerful horn blast from a taxi arriving outside. She opens her eyes, springs up, checks her appearance in a mirror, makes a final adjustment to the angle of an item on

*a shelf. There's a loud, impatient ring on the doorbell. Olive takes
a deep breath. She faces down stage, and, using her right index
finger, makes a jerky little circle in the area of her heart, anti-
clockwise*

One-two. One-two. One-two.

This fortifying ritual completed, Olive exits to open the door

Monica (*off*) About time! I'm getting drenched out here!
Olive (*off*) Hiya. Come on in.

*Olive enters, followed by Ernest. He is carrying an extremely
large pair of suitcases. Olive is carrying a slighter smaller one*

I'm so glad you were able to spot her, Ernest.
Ernest Hasn't she great luggage and you after telling me she was
  only planning to stay a couple of weeks. Where do you want
  these settled?
Olive Ah, just put them down there, Ernest. Tell me now, are you
  still going to lend us your you-know-what?
Ernest Course I am. Amn't I a man of my word? And here she is.

Monica enters, carrying a vanity case and handbag

Monica (*briskly*) Why don't we get Ernest to put my things
  straight into my room.
Olive This *is* your room.

Monica looks around, takes everything in

Monica Ah.
Ernest Well, I'll be off, then, ladies. I'm sure you've loads to
  chat about and you apart seven years.

Olive Right you are, Ernest. See you soon.

There's an awkward pause

Ernest Will you settle up now like, or…
Monica Oh, of course. Could you sort it out for me, Olive, I've no Irish currency yet. Seven pounds, I think. Give him eight, would you. He was a lamb about the bags.

After a slight hesitation, Olive stands on a footstool, reaches to the top shelf of a bookcase and lifts down a stone jar. She rummages in it and gives Ernest the taxi fare

Olive There you go, Ernest. Thanks very much. And drive carefully.
Ernest Lovely, Olive. Take care yourself now. (*He extends his hand to Monica*)

She is engaged in examining the room and doesn't notice it

Olive Ernest is saying goodbye, Monica.

Monica turns, shakes Ernest's hand briefly, barely looking at him

Monica Off you go, Ernest. Thanks for the non-stop commentary.

Ernest begins to back out

Ernest See you, Olive.
Olive See you, Ernest.

Ernest exits

Ernest (*off*) See you, Hilary.

Hilary (*off*) Drive carefully, Ernest.

Monica picks up a chunk of semi-precious stone, feels its weight

Olive We found that on a walk recently. Great vibes, very unusual.
Monica Is that so? It could be cut up for jewellery. Well, let's have a look at you. (*She pauses*) You certainly look … healthy. Interesting hair colour.
Olive Thank you. Hilary does it. And I do hers. We use vegetable dyes. We make them ourselves. Of course, they're not very long-lasting, so we have to do it once a week. But who cares, we have plenty of time. Another small disadvantage is that it comes off a bit. But we don't mind that either, because most of our clothes and bedlinen and stuff are dyed too. Hilary's in a purple phase, but I'm still in my pink cycle. (*She pats her hair*) Glad you like it.
Monica What's your real colour these days?
Olive I'm pure white under all this. I suppose you are too?
Monica White—at my age? You're joking, of course.

We hear the loud clatter of a dropped saucepan

Hilary (*off*) Oh—*ships!*
Olive That's Hilary. She's been dropping stuff all day. She's low on magnesium. I'll just make a note. (*She scribbles on a pad. She calls out*) OK, Hilary?

Hilary enters, wearing large oven gloves

Hilary Sorry about the racket, girls. The handle came off that bloody saucepan again. We'll have to get it welded. Welcome, Monica. God! I'd have known you anywhere. Look at the two of you. Twins!

*Monica looks from beaming Olive to her own reflection in the
mirror*

Monica I've never been able to see it myself.
Hilary It's all in the skeleton. The spitting image. So how's
    London?
Monica Noisy. Over-crowded. Over-run with foreigners. Rub-
    bish everywhere. One can't walk down the street for old
    mattresses and kitchen units.
Olive We'd love an old kitchen unit, wouldn't we, Hilary? In
    fact, I wouldn't say no to a mattress. My futon's beginning to
    feel like a half empty sack of potatoes.
Hilary I warned her about washing it, but she wouldn't listen.
    She hosed it down in the garden on the first day of spring and
    the filling went into spasm. Anyway, Mon, sit down and make
    yourself at home. I'll join you later. I have to get the lentils back
    into the saucepan before they become a permanent fixture on
    the floor. There's home-made wine there. Help yourself, it'll
    sharpen your appetite.
Monica Don't worry about dinner for me. I had a bite on the
    plane.
Hilary No problem. I'll put your portion aside till you're
    peckish.

Hilary exits

Monica She seems a nice sort of woman. Have you been sharing
    long?
Olive Over a year now. She's terrific. Always so good-natured.
    We've never had a cross word. Not once.
Monica Sounds idyllic. Wish I could say the same about Derek.
    I can't remember the last time we had a civil conversation. He's
    suddenly decided I cramp his creativity. Always going on

about peace and quiet. Well, now he's got it, and good luck to him! (*She carelessly shoves a number of crystals aside, to make space for her vanity case on a shelf*)

Olive moves forward protectively, but doesn't complain

Olive So he didn't mind you taking off for a bit.
Monica I didn't give him the option. He's no idea where I've gone. Let him stew in it, that's what I say. When he rings here, desperate to reach me, you're not to say you've heard from me. You won't believe what he's done. Resigned from a perfectly good, pensionable job at ICI, because he wants to work with chairs. Not shares. Chairs. The flat is littered with prototypes—not one of them fit to sit on. God knows what's come over him. He actually believes he has a talent for it. Well, I've had enough. I'm tired of being a people-pleaser.
Olive (*uncertainly*) A people-pleaser?
Monica Years of knocking myself out to oblige everybody else, with my own needs at the bottom of the list. A born people-pleaser my whole life—but all that's going to change.
Olive How long do you expect to be away?
Monica Open ticket.

Olive pours wine into two glasses

Hardly any for me, thanks. My dermatologist says I should cut down on alcohol.

Olive pours two full glasses

Olive This hasn't even started fermenting yet. We only made it last night. Look at the state of my feet. (*She pulls down one of her socks, revealing a red stained ankle*)

Monica Good God. Won't it wash off?

Olive Ah, it will. But the boiler only produces enough water for one bath a day and it was Hilary's turn. I'm a bit worried about Derek, though. Did you leave him a note, so he'll know you're OK?

Monica I left him all the usual instructions.

Olive That's great so. As long as he knows you left on purpose. (*She pauses*) If you don't mind my saying so, Monica, you seem very tense.

Monica Can you blame me? My bloody life's a complete shambles. I might as well be dead! Years of being a devoted wife and suddenly I'm expected to economise while that lunatic builds crooked furniture. It's the old story. People-pleasers get walked all over. (*She gets out a packet of cigarettes*)

Olive Oh, sorry, but Hilary and I have sort of banned that. The rooms are so small, you see. It's as if we'd *all* be smoking, if you were. You could pop out into the garden, if you're desperate.

Monica And catch my death? No, thanks. (*She sighs heavily and puts the cigarettes away*)

Olive You're so full of tension and negative thoughts, your aura's positively spiky. Try this: (*she demonstrates her anti-clockwise movement*) one-two. One-two. One-two.

Monica What the hell is that suppose to do?

Olive The body's energy is a dynamic spiral travelling up clockwise from your feet to the top of your head. When negativity gets a grip, the spiral is disrupted. So you have to ease out the kink with an anti-clockwise movement in the region of your heart. (*She demonstrates again*) One-*two*. One-*two*. One-*two*.

Monica Are you winding me up?

Olive Try it. Just try it, and you'll feel better immediately. (*She demonstrates again*)

Monica Don't be childish, Olive.

Olive Just try it. It's physical rather than spiritual, so it's effective whether you believe in it or not. Go on, have a go.

Monica Another time, Olive. I'm not up to hocus pocus right now. Anyway, when did you get into all this stuff? These lumps of glass or whatever they are?

Olive Those are vibrating rocks and crystals. Hilary and I are considered important collectors.

Hilary (*off*) Grub's up. Make space!

Olive clears a space on the floor, then exits to the kitchen

Monica looks after her, then begins to perform the anti-clockwise movement as demonstrated. She fails to complete it, makes a dismissive gesture

Olive and Hilary enter, each carrying a large wooden salad bowl. They sit on the floor, cross-legged, facing each other

Olive reaches over to a cassette player and switches it on. We hear formless whiny music with an oriental feel to it. Olive and Hilary each take a wooden spoon from their bowl and pause, waiting for a particular passage of music. When it comes, they touch spoons and begin to eat rhythmically, looking at each other. They chew with great care and tilt back their heads each time they swallow. Monica peers at the contents of Olive's bowl, leans in to sniff at it, recoils

Monica What in God's name are you eating?

Olive mimes that when they eat, they do not talk and vice versa

(*Following the mime, supplying words*) When you eat … you don't talk … and when you talk … you don't eat. (*She shakes her head silently, sits down. She opens her vanity case and takes out a long emery board. She files her nails, briskly at first and then at the pace dictated by the music)*

Slow fade to black

SCENE 2

The next morning

Hilary enters the darkened room, carrying a mug of tea. She opens the curtains, flooding the room with light. She is wearing another set of purple clothes and knitted gloves with the tops of the fingers cut off

Monica is fast asleep on her futon, formerly the sofa. She has used various items from her luggage to supplement her bedding. At the begining of the scene, the futon area is concealed by a folding screen, decorated with pictures of angels

Hilary Wakey-uppy. It's nearly ten and Olive will need the room. She's expecting a client. Here you are now: a nice cup of nettle tea to get you going. Would you like an egg?

Monica Is there something wrong with the heating, Hilary. I thought I was going to freeze solid during the night.

Hilary Oh sorry, we should've warned you. We're out of fuel at the moment, so it's back to the old two-bar, I'm afraid.

She folds back the screen, revealing Monica sitting up in bed and wearing a luxuriously thick, white bathrobe. Monica tastes her tea, hastily puts it aside and retreats back under the bedclothes

Sorry, Mon, but you'll have to get up. Hop into Olive's bed if you want to sleep on. But don't speak to her. She's meditating at the moment. She likes a little meditate before a reading.

Monica gets up, starts pulling on clothes beneath her dressing gown

Monica (*very bad-tempered*) A reading of *what*?

Hilary rolls up the futon

Hilary Probably the Tarots, although sometimes she prefers the runes. Depends on the client's vibes.
Monica You're not telling me she's a fortune teller.
Hilary Oh no. Olive's a psychic. Very well known, actually. Nobody around here would make a move without her.

Olive enters, wearing a huge pink cloak, crudely fashioned from a blanket. It has an elasticated neck and stand-up collar

Aha. Speak of the devil...
Olive Hi, Monica. Sorry to rush you, but I need the room.

Moving swiftly, Olive piles Monica's things on to a rug, rolls it up and exits with it. She returns immediately and unfolds the screen, so that Monica and the futon are concealed again

Olive climbs on to the footstool, lifts down the stone jar and a kitchen timer and places them near a small table. She clocks the rocks and crystals, performs a rapid anti-clockwise movement, makes a minute adjustment to an arrangement. She raises her hand for silence. We hear nothing

He's here. His aura is red. He is a ... gingerbread man.

Hilary shakes her head, clearly filled with admiration

The doorbell rings

Hilary exits to answer it

Olive sits at the small table, lights a stick of incense, bows her head

Bernard enters nervously. He is middle-aged and dressed entirely in ginger brown clothing, in an outfit topped by a large, long ginger coat. Even his skin has a gingerish tinge

Olive silently indicates the empty chair across the table. Bernard removes his cap and sits. Olive looks at him, then reaches for a deck of Tarot cards

What is your question?
Bernard (*whispering*) How much is it?

Olives reaches over to a picture on the wall, flips it back to front. A hand-painted legend reads:

> *"please indicate*
> *Short term £5*
> *Long term £8*
> *(or payment in kind)"*

Bernard puts his index finger firmly on the £5. Olive nods serenely and indicates the stone jar. With shaking hands, Bernard deposits five pounds in it

Olive Thank you. What is your question?
Bernard I can't make up my mind, like. I can't sleep for trying

to make the right decision. I have to let them know by tomorrow, like.

Nodding encouragingly, Olive deals out a few Tarot cards. Behind the screen, Monica listens intently. She gets out a cigarette, remembers she can't smoke, throws the cigarette aside crossly

Olive I sense a dilemma concerning your job.
Bernard (*thrilled*) Jaysus, aren't you great, and me hardly saying a word yet. That's right, missus. My job's the root of the problem. Even after fifteen years I'm like an round peg in a——
Olive You are unhappy with your choice of career. You feel drawn to something quite different. I feel a great struggle within you.

Bernard nods frantically. Monica reacts with scorn

Bernard It was reading about Bernard Farrell that did it. He worked at Sealink for fifteen years before he found the courage to leave and write his plays in earnest. And look at him today. A great fella altogether. Now I'm not saying I could write one straight off like he does, but how will I know if I don't give it a try. Isn't it true for me?
Olive You have always suppressed your creative side...

Bernard slaps his thigh, delighted

You have toiled in an atmosphere that has nourished your body, but failed to nourish your spirit.

Monica makes a gagging gesture

Bernard Exactly, missus, exactly.

Olive Your dilemma is whether to give notice. To give up a job that has sustained you well in some ways, but failed you in others...

Bernard That's it exactly, *exactly*. I could take early retirement like, and get a golden handshake. Or I could wait five years on full salary and *then* retire. But I'm stuck, like. Is it lack of courage, do you think? Would you say I'm a coward? The wee house goes with the job, you see. And I've the wife and four girls still in school, God bless them. Then again, there's fellas making fortunes out of writing plays. His nibs, Tom Murphy, and your man who died, Sam Beckett. Sure there's even women at it and they all driving around in big cars and their picture in the papers. I've great stories in me. About going to school in my bare feet, without as much as a crust for my lunch. And the time my auntie saw the Devil's face in the clouds at Salthill. Sure I could describe unusual events concerning a certain Christian Brother... *Not* that I'm saying I would. I only mentioned it to demonstrate that I'm never stuck for a good plot, like.

Olive gently raises her hand to silence him

(*Continuing in a whisper*) —And then me and that Farrell fella have the same Christian name. Would that be an omen?

Olive consults the cards

Olive Is your name... Bernard?

Bernard throws up his hands, overwhelmed with amazement

I see a five year period of intense endeavour, in which you continue to nourish your body—but with an eye on your soul.

Bernard (*concentrating intensely*)...Soul.

Olive During this period you will see many plays, read many books. You will be gathering your resources, enriching your inner self, letting your creative juices collect in an almighty dam.

Bernard …Dam.

Olive And when the time is right, about five years hence, you will be ready to begin. Your angel is Allana-ladda.

Bernard Alan Ladd? Your man the film star?

Olive Allana-ladda. He who moves in a reddish brown mist. Allana-ladda will take you by the hand when the time is right. It's all here, clear as crystal.

The timer buzzes noisily. Olive gathers the cards and puts them aside

Bernard Well, aren't you a bloody wonder when all's said and done. Haven't you a real gift. I feel a great weight off my mind. I'll sleep like a top tonight, so I will. A million thanks, missus. Oh, just one other thing…

Olive Certainly.

Bernard When the five years is up and Allana-ladda gives me his hand, do you see any sign of like, progress, in the play writing department. Anything up on a poster, for instance. That sort of thing.

Olive spreads the cards again

Olive (*slowly*) I see a bea——

Bernard Ah bee. Abbey. Jaysus, is it the Abbey you see?

Olive I see a beaming postman approaching your door many, many times. He always carries a large brown envelope. That's all I can say for the moment.

Monica conceals her laughter. Olive sits back, closes her eyes.

Bernard rummages in his wallet, puts a second five pound note into the jar

Bernard I'm privileged to add a bit extra, missus. You've unplucked me from the horns of a dilemma, as Shakespeare might say. More power to you and your great work. Thanks very much. Thanks very much.

Bernard exits jauntily, a new man

Monica emerges from behind the screen

Monica Well! Talk about money for jam. Hey—wake up, he's gone.

Olive doesn't respond

Hilary enters, urgently hushes Monica

Hilary Sshh. She needs a few minutes to recover after a reading. It takes it out of her.
Monica Relax, girls. The punter's gone. Nice going, Olive. And tax free.

Olive stands. Hilary clears the way for her departure, reverently touches Olive's back as she passes

Olive exits as if entranced

As soon as Olive's exit is complete, Hilary briskly extinguishes the incense stick and puts away the screen, cards, etc.

Hilary She'll be fine in just a moment.

Monica Is this for real? My sister the psychic. How long's this
lot been going on?
Hilary I think the first time she was guided by her angel was
about four years ago. Audio-murphino, his name is, told her
that she had the gift. She resigned from her job as a legal
secretary and gave all her power suits and high heels to a jumble
sale. And she's never looked back, God bless her. I'm the same.
I was a solicitor before I saw the light. I'm in a five year cycle,
growing organic vegetables, as instructed by Yulo-Brynnero.
Monica Your guardian angel, right?
Hilary We prefer to call them *guiding* angels. Olive's the main
channel. All angels are appointed through Olive. I can't tell you
how easy life's become. Our zucchinis are the size of marrows
since Yulo-Brynnero guided us to the coal horse.

We hear the clippity clop of a horse in the street outside, then a
whistle, a snort and whinny

Monica (*brightening*) Does this mean we'll have heat?
Hilary Well, no. As I said, we're a bit short of funds at the
moment. It's the manure I'm after. Excuse me now, would you,
Mon. It's at its most potent when it's really fresh. (*She moves*
as if to exit, then hesitates) Ah, what the hell. We'll lash out and
get a bag of coal in honour of our guest.

Hilary takes some money out of the stone jar and exits

Olive enters in yesterday's clothes

Olive Hi again. Have you had your breakfast? We have free-
range eggs and lovely black bread... Or, we have yoghurt?
Monica (*hopefully*) In a little carton? Shop-bought yoghurt?
Olive Yep.

Olive exits and returns instantly with a carton of yoghurt and a small wooden spoon

Monica tucks into the yoghurt with difficulty, as the bowl of the spoon is too wide. Finally she uses the handle. She is starving and finishes the carton very quickly

Monica So. Hilary was telling me how you've developed this fortune telling thing.

Olive I don't tell fortunes. I'm just the medium between caring angels and people in need of guidance.

Monica Come off it, Olly. This is me. Your sister. *Family.* If you want to throw away years of education and do this stuff, OK. But don't feed me that psychic garbage.

Olive I'm used to sceptics. Denying the spiritual is entirely up to the individual. All I can say is, I've been chosen as a medium and I've never been happier. Hilary and I have achieved perfect peace. We have a safe home, we're never short of food, we're never ill—not even a headache. You ought to try it, at least while you're here. You're still very tense.

Monica (*snapping*) I am not a bit tense. It's a shock to visit your sister and find her behaving like some gypsy throwback. Tarot cards. Wooden spoons. Give me a break!

Olive Our angels have advised us to dispense with metal cutlery, except for our knife. The Tarot cards are simply a prop to relax people in need of guidance.

Monica In need of having their heads read. I wish your angel would advise you on central heating. And a bit of make-up wouldn't go amiss. Look at your skin—I bet you haven't had a facial in years. And your finger nails are like … like *shovels*.

Olive Our nails re-generate at exactly the right pace for the life we lead. With sensitive equipment you could hear your nails screaming with pain as you file them. Hair's the same, so we only cut off the dead bits at the end of their cycle. It's obvious really, when you think about it.

Monica Jesus wept. I suppose you have a pair of forests in your armpits. Yuk!

Olive We always smell lovely because we cleanse our bodies with rain dampened herbs. Our bath water comes from a rain-fed cistern. We never run out, even in summer.

Hilary enters with a pile of white pillowcases, and a large sack of dried herbs

Hilary Are you hot to trot, Ol?

Olive Yeah—we better get cracking. We need at least two dozen for Saturday.

Monica Don't tell me. To supplement the readings you have a nice little earner in arts and crafts.

Olive and Hilary exchange glances, perform a rapid anti-clockwise

Hilary (*smiling*) Herb pillows. Lavender, thyme, camomile, and so on. You don't know what deep, refreshing sleep is until you've tried one. (*She stuffs a pillowcase expertly, zips up the opening, moves on to another*)

Olive does the same. Monica picks up a stuffed pillow, holds it to her cheek

Monica Nobody could sleep on this. You can feel the thorns and stuff.

Olive Only for a moment or two. Then you're out like a light.

Hilary Would you like to do a few? We need loads for our stall at the market on Saturday.

Monica How much do they sell for?

Olive Five pounds for one, nine for two, twelve for three and so on. We get the material and zippers from a factory in exchange for corporate readings. We grow some of the herbs ourselves and supplement with wild ones. We can't keep up with the demand. Aren't we great!

Monica I'm impressed. *Very* impressed. Of course, you could add a bit of lace and sell them for twenty.

Olive and Hilary pause in their work, perform an anti-clockwise and resume

What's the matter, girls, did I say something commercial? Heaven forbid you should make a few pounds! Isn't there a shop you could supply, one of those silly places featuring barrels of pot pourri? They'd go big on this. Let's see … you could call them Sweet Dreams, gift wrap them. They ought to be boxed with a cellophane lid and a nice bow. Have you thought of mail order?

Olive You're still in marketing, then?

Monica Look, if you really want to know, I'm going through a pretty bad patch. Married to a madman without a shred of ambition——

Olive (*to Hilary*) He escaped from accountancy into chair design.

Hilary Lovely.

Monica —Sick of my friends. Sick of living in London. Scared of getting old. I'll be honest, I need a change, a bit of a challenge.

Hilary So you decided to take a little holiday?

Monica I just dropped everything and took off. Partly to teach Derek a lesson. You know, it's hard to believe, but sometimes I think he imagines he could manage without me. A man who can barely use a bloody microwave.

Olive He'll probably surprise himself. Cooking's a piece of cake as long as you simplify it and stick to essentials.

Monica Speaking of food. I hate to eat alone, so how about you guys joining me for dinner tonight.

Olive Sorry, Monica, but Hilary and I never eat out.

Monica Don't tell me: your angels wouldn't approve.

Hilary Restaurant food is full of artificial colourants and preservatives. That's why rich people are generally more neurotic than poor people. Because of eating out more, slowly poisoning themselves.

Olive In any case, you ought to stick around this evening. Ernest is bringing over his pyramid. It's brilliant. Really powerful. He's letting us borrow it for a bit.

Monica You socialise with Ernest the taxi driver?

Hilary Ernest is one of our closest friends. His angel is Gregorius-Peckus, a reformed fallen. Ernest is living his nineteenth earthly life, so his powers are nearly at peak. Didn't you notice the light in his eye?

Monica joins them and stuffs a pillowcase

Monica Only when he was hanging around for his tip. Speaking of friends, are either if you seeing anybody? Romantically, I mean?

Hilary (*laughing*) Indeed we're not! Sure there's no men around here. The married ones can't get divorced and bachelors of our age are just looking for housekeepers. No. We dispensed with men about the same time we gave up meat. Now we just see them as human beings of another gender.

Olive We gave up meat and men on the first Monday in May. And we've never regretted it.

Monica You don't miss sex at all?

Olive Well, even when I was getting it, I was missing it, if you know what I mean. Sure it's all in the mind.

Monica Rubbish. If a couple of hunks turned up, you'd soon rethink all that. I mean you're not unattractive. (*She brightens*) How about letting me make you over? Image building is my main talent. Now *that* would be a challenge worth tackling. A little weight loss here, a supportive bra there. You wouldn't know yourselves. Then we could market the Sweet Dreams in a business-like way and before you know it... (*She spreads her hands expansively*)
Olive That's very kind of you, Monica, but it's taken us ages to achieve what we have now. Thanks very much for the thought, though.
Hilary Yes, thanks very much.

Monica handles a pillow thoughtfully, sniffs it. Olive and Hilary begin to sing a cheerful Irish folk song, harmonising charmingly

Fade to black

Scene 3

Evening, the same day

The pillows have been cleared away

Monica, dressed as in Scene 2, except for a different jacket, is adjusting her make-up at the mirror

Hilary enters with four long white candles and matches, puts them on the floor. She clears a section of floor space L, then paces, making sure the space will accommodate a structure about three feet square

Monica sneaks up on her and sprays her with perfume. Hilary springs back, coughing and waving her hands

Hilary What in the name of God...

Monica Chanel Number Five.

Hilary It's disgusting! Imagine wanting to spray yourself with chemicals and musk.

Monica Gorgeous. And I can get it for next to nothing through an old marketing connection. I've had the most *brilliant* idea. I sprayed a little in your sackful of Sweet Slumbers.

Hilary (*faintly*) Jesus, Mary and Joseph. Tell me you're joking.

Monica Wait till you see what it does for business.

Hilary We'll have to burn the lot. A week's working, counting the sewing. (*She looks cross, performs an anti-clockwise, recovers her good nature immediately*) Ah well.

Monica Listen, Hilary, I've been wanting to speak to you, privately. If you don't mind my saying so, I think you're letting Olive dominate you a bit too much. I mean, let's face it, you've got a degree in law, for God's sake. And now you stuff pillows. What a waste of a brain. It's different for Olive. She always was a little flaky. She believed in Santa till she was fourteen years old, collected pictures of fairies till she was in her twenties.

Hilary Forgive me for saying this, Monica, but you don't really know her. She's one of the most intelligent people I've ever met. She knows exactly how she wants to live. I've never known anyone so happy, and I'm the same.

Monica A carbon copy, that's what you are. You're not the hairy-armpits type, Hilary. Living in this cramped little excuse for a house isn't for you. Come on, don't be scared to face it. It's been an interesting phase and now you're just the teeniest bit sick of it, yes?

Hilary (*uncomfortably*) I don't know what you mean. I love our house and garden. Practising law was sheer hell. I was miserable. I couldn't sleep without pills, I ate rich food and got migraine. I thank the Lord for the day Olive turned up as a temp. If I hadn't met her I'd be...

Monica Well-to-do and successful. Think about it, that's all I'm saying. Would it be so terrible to meet a nice guy, someone who'd take care of you in your old age, give you a bit of status in the community. Don't be a people-pleaser like I was. Promise me you'll just think about it.

Hilary OK, I'll think about it.

Monica Now you're talking. A few years back, I saved my husband in exactly the same way. He had this crazy idea about opening a little coffee shop. "Le Rive Gauche" he wanted to call it. Had plans for sitting around all day, chatting to people and reading foreign newspapers. Thanks to me, he saw the light and stuck to accountancy. This time round I'm going to be very firm. He'll be grateful in the long run.

Hilary But he's obviously not happy with accountancy.

Monica Who's happy? It's the twentieth century, living with stress is being *alive*.

Hilary Well, I dunno, Monica...

Monica Wait a minute... (*She rummages in a suitcase, withdraws a huge silk scarf*) Here. Swap that itchy-looking thing for this. Remember soft, sensual fabrics? (*She whips off Hilary's shawl, replaces it with the scarf, which she drapes artfully. She places Hilary in front of the mirror*) Well. Look at you.

Hilary I must say the colour suits me. Gorgeous. Pure silk, I bet you.

Monica Of course.

Hilary Well, maybe just for this evening. Thanks.

Monica My pleasure. Tomorrow we'll have a leg-shaving ceremony and get you into a pair of tights. I bet you haven't seen the skin of your legs for years.

The doorbell rings

Olive (*off*) Hiya, Ernest. Bring it in. Bring it in. I'll give you a hand.

Olive and Ernest enter, carrying eight long poles. Ernest also carries a pyramid-shaped parcel wrapped in brown paper and a tartan shopping bag, which he handles with great care

Ernest Evening, ladies. Ready for the experience of a lifetime?

Ernest and Olive sniff, looking disgusted

Hilary Chanel Number Five.

Olive notices Hilary's silk scarf. She moves to the discarded shawl, picks it up, folds it carefully

It's so good of you to lend us something so precious, Ernest. We'll be really careful with it.
Ernest Don't mention it. The truth is, they're inclined to withdraw if they're left alone, so you'll be doing me a favour.
Monica What is it, a home gymnasium sort of thing?
Ernest (*smiling*) Not a home gymnasium, no.
Olive Just wait and see, Monica. You're in for a real treat!

Ernest assembles the pyramid. First he positions the four base poles, then he slots in the four corner poles. Finally he unwraps the brown paper parcel and puts the pyramid peak in place, completing the structure

Hilary (*softly*) Will we light the candles, Ernest?
Ernest If you would.

Olive and Hilary light the candles and position them at two corners of the pyramid. Olive puts on a cassette and we hear strange, mystical music. Hilary dims the lights. With great ceremony, Ernest takes a smooth dark stone about the size of a

*rugby ball from the shopping bag. It glistens in the candlelight.
Olive and Hilary gasp*

Olive My God, Ernest! What a beauty! Where did you get it?
Ernest The quarry. I went down one evening after they'd been
    blasting, and there it was.
Monica What makes it shine that way?
Ernest Pure essence of angel. Probably a third century fallen
    awakened by the San Francisco earthquake.
Monica (*muttering*) Give me strength!
Olive Is he named?
Ernest Oh yes. Gregorius-Peckus introduced us almost imme-
    diately. Orsinara-wella-wella. Can you feel the power, ladies?
Monica I hope it's not bloody well radioactive. We could all end
    up with bald heads.

Pause

Ernest Your sister's still without a guide, then, Olive?
Olive Still resisting. You can't rush these things, Ernest. You
    know how it is.
Ernest Certainly I do. Now: will I give ye a demonstration?

Olive and Hilary nod eagerly

    You first, Hilary.

*Ernest leads Hilary into the pyramid, sits her down. Then places
the rock inside the pyramid, in front of her. Hilary holds her head
slightly to one side, a little stiffly. All is silent, then the rock begins
to tick slowly. Hilary shivers with pleasure, closes her eyes*

Monica (*suspiciously*) Hang on, hang on. I saw something like
    this in that film *Cocoon*.

Olive ⎫
Ernest ⎭ (*together*) Sshhh.

Hilary Hello, Mr Wella-wella... Orsinara, then, thank you very much... I'm fine, thank you. (*She listens, nodding and smiling*) Well, it's very kind of you to say so. (*She listens*) Oh, it's just a stiff neck—I probably slept at an awkward angle. (*She listens, then slowly straightens her neck. She wiggles her head, demonstrating that the stiffness has gone*) Oh, aren't you great, it's good as new. (*She listens*) I will indeed. Thanks very much. (*She opens her eyes and climbs out of the pyramid, all smiles*)

Ernest Now you, Olive.

Olive hops into the pyramid. The rock glows afresh

Olive Good evening, Orsinara. This is Olive speaking. (*She listens*) I know you're not a telephone. It's just force of habit. (*She listens, then begins to laugh helplessly*)

Ernest and Hilary join in. Monica tries hard to resist, but smiles despite herself. Olive slaps her knees, bursting with amusement. She quietens, listens carefully

OK and thanks a million. We're honoured to have you in the house. (*She listens*) Bye now.

The ticking stops. Olive opens her eyes and climbs out

He's marvellous. A real find. Great sense of humour.

Monica So what was so funny?

Olive It's impossible to explain. I just had a feeling of absolute well-being. Pure joy.

Hilary Bliss.

Ernest That's the ticket. And what about yourself, Monica? Step in and see what happens.

Monica Here I go. People-pleasing again. (*She climbs into the*

pyramid, sits down, closes her eyes, waits. She cups one ear as if listening, then the other) Anybody home?
Olive Try not to mock, Monica. Just let him find your channel. Breathe in and out slowly. Be receptive.

Olive, Hilary and Ernest hum softly. A long, low note. The peace is broken by the anguished howl of a dog. Monica springs out of the pyramid, switches on the light

Monica Bloody hell!
Olive It was only a dog out in the street, Monica. No reason to get alarmed.
Ernest Don't despair. When you're properly receptive, your angel will reach out to you. The vibrations in this house are first class. You'll be as privileged as we are in no time.
Monica Don't hold your breath.

Pause

Ernest Well, I'd better wend my way. I'll send ye a card, girls.
Hilary I'll see you out to the car, Ernest.

He shakes hands with Olive and Monica

Ernest Oh—a little moisture now and then, if you'd be so kind. He's been used to damp, in the quarry.
Olive Right you are, Ernest. Safe journey.

Ernest and Hilary exit

Olive gazes at the pyramid, full of admiration

Monica I hope I'm not expected to sleep in the same room as that heap of junk.

Olive performs a swift anti-clockwise

Olive Actually, you'll never be safer. A reformed fallen is as good as gold. I've never heard of a reformed abusing its powers.

Monica For goodness sake, Olive! Hearing you sprout that junk is positively embarrassing. It's time we had a talk. In fact, I've been dying for a chance to get you alone. During the last couple of days, I've observed the dynamics of this household and I have to tell you I don't like what I see. You seem to be hopping about like a puppet at her beck and call.

Olive But we couldn't be happ——

Monica Yes, I know you think you're happy, but I'm seeing things with a fresh eye. If you weren't my own flesh and blood, I'd write you off as a bit touched. Thank God I arrived when I did, in time to save you from getting any deeper into all this psychic crap.

Olive performs an anti-clockwise

And stop doing that. It's driving me crazy.

Olive I wouldn't dream of telling you how to live. Please don't interfere with my lifestyle.

Monica What "lifestyle"? Haven't you noticed that you do all the dirty work around here. OK, she cooks—if you can call it cooking—but you do all the cleaning up. You stuff four cushion to her one. She seems a nice person, but she's totally misguided and wants you as a companion for God knows what peculiar reason… No make-up. No meat. No *men*, for Pete's sake. What kind of lifestyle is that? I'm sure your neighbours think you're a pair of lesbians.

Olive turns aside and performs a discreet anti-clockwise

And another thing: these cranks you're hanging out with. All *her* friends, right?

Olive Hilary's more outgoing than I am. People are drawn to her. We share everything, including our friends.

Monica I've never seen *her* putting money in the little brown jug. You have to bust your brain telling fortunes while she sits around raking it in.

Olive Speaking of the jug, do you think you could pay back the eight for the taxi and the ten you borrowed on Monday. I hate to ask, but Hilary needs a new hoe.

Monica Don't attempt to divert me with trivia. You're being taken for a ride and you can't see it. Well, I'm taking over from now on. You'll end up thanking me, mark my words.

Olive Monica, I think you better leave. You're not comfortable here and there's a lovely little bed and breakfast up the road. With central heating. Or maybe you should think about going home to Derek, give it another try.

Monica I spoke to that half-wit last night. He's still persevering with his idiotic plans and I'm certainly not going back till he sees the light. I'm prepared to stick it out here for your sake. First I'll sort you out, then I'll attend to my own needs. I owe it to you, I'm the only family you've got.

Olive I don't want Hilary upset. She's had a tough life and she's just begun to find happiness.

Monica Yeah—she was very happy when I agreed to lend her my silk scarf. Her eyes bug out every time I open one of my suitcases. Don't be a mug, Olly, it's not too late. You could take a word processing course, sign on with one of those Empty Nest Returner's Employment Agencies.

Olive But my nest isn't a bit empty. And I don't want to return. I just got here.

Monica begins to undress, going behind the screen. She emerges in her white towelling bathrobe

Monica Look: I wasn't going to tell you this, but perhaps it's better if I do. I had a little chat with Hilary and she confided in me that she's pretty sick of all this. You watch—one of these days she'll get herself a fat job in corporate law and leave you high and dry with your pillows and Tarot cards. Think about it. I'm going to grab a bath—and don't tell me it's Hilary's turn. It *always* seems to be Hilary's turn.

Monica exits

Olive stands alone, c. She looks around the room, trying to draw comfort from it. She approaches the mirror and sadly studies her reflection. The Lights dim on their own. The candles continue to burn. The rock begins to tick. Olive approaches the pyramid, pauses, then steps inside and sits as before. After a period of listening and nodding, she begins to smile. She climbs out of the pyramid, finds Monica's handbag, takes out a packet of cigarettes and places it in the pyramid

Still smiling thoughtfully, Olive exits

SCENE 4

Monica enters, fresh from her bath, whistling cheerfully. She rolls out her futon, and after a furtive look towards the exit, searches for her cigarettes with increasing urgency. She is about to search a suitcase when she spots the cigarettes in the pyramid. After a moment of confusion, she smiles

Monica So smoking is permitted after all. Good on you, Olly, you're getting the message. (*She goes to the pyramid, reaches for the packet*)

It moves out of reach. Startled, she snatches back her hand. She tries again. Once more the packet moves

Now don't be greedy. If you want a little smoke, I'll be happy to breathe on you, OK. (*She steps into the pyramid, sits and lights a cigarette. She blows smoke on to the rock*) Good boy, rocky. Takes you back to your pre-reformed days, yeah? (*She laughs*)

The rock ticks

OK. Very clever. Now let's find out what makes you tick. (*She reaches for the rock, withdraws her hand on finding it hot. A little uneasy, she draws on her cigarette, shows signs of being uncomfortably warm*) Jesus, you either freeze or bake in this madhouse. (*She stubs her cigarette out on the rock and moves to leave the pyramid. She mimes hitting an obstruction with her head and we hear a muffled thud. She rubs her head*) Hey! (*She tries to leave the pyramid, once again encounters an invisible obstruction*)

We hear another thud. The ticking gives way to an eerie, high-pitched keening and the rushing sound of beating wings

(*In pain*) Bloody hell Olive!

It's as if there are walls of glass between the poles. She moves her hands over the surfaces, finds all exits blocked. Monica panics, begins to thump and kick and shoulder the walls. Each movement is choreographed to a sound effect. She shouts for help. Her voice is heard distantly, becoming fainter and fainter. Our final image of her is not unlike a Frances Bacon painting. She screams silently, her face contorted with terror

Olive! Help! Somebody help me. **Help meeeeeeee…**

The sound effect ends and Monica's scream stops abruptly

Black-out

SCENE 5

Early evening, a few days later

The pyramid is still in position, but completely covered with Olive's big pink cloak

Olive is fiddling with the cassette player. Her dress style is now a mixture of New Age and city chic. She wears the silk scarf and her footwear has been replaced with knee length suede boots. She lights a stick of incense and puts on a cassette

Hilary (*off*) Are you hot to trot, Ol?
Olive (*happily*) Starving, Hilary. (*She starts the eating music and it plays softly*)

Hilary enters with the wooden bowls. She too, has adopted a mixture of styles, most noticeably in her smart tan shoes and tights and a Chanel-style chain belt

Both women wear several items of bold costume jewellery. Hilary puts the bowls on what seems to be a low table, covered with a white sheet. Olive pours two glasses of wine

Hilary Here we are.
Olive That smells good. What are we having?

Hilary Noodles with cashew nuts. With chilled melon for desert, followed by a cup of cereal coffee and a KitKat each.

Olive Perfection. Although ... maybe we should keep the KitKats till later, to have with our Horlicks.

Hilary Good thinking. How did your five o'clock reading go?

Olive Lovely. The client was worried that her husband would find out she'd had a little fling. But I was able to reassure her that she had nothing to worry about. The husband was in yesterday, worrying about the same thing.

Hilary So are the pair of them going to mend their ways?

Olive I advised them to make an effort to be kind and loving to each other. To pretend they're not married, in other words. They'll be nice out of guilt to begin with, but there's always the chance they'll start enjoying each other again.

Hilary You're brilliant, so y'are Olive. Brilliant.

Olive How's the new hoe?

Hilary A thing of joy. Lovely long handle on it. I think I'll keep it well scrubbed. Wooden handles are lovely when they're new.

Olive That's true. Although old ones are nice too. They give off more vibes when they're old. Take on a nice patina.

Hilary Yes. You're right. They *do* get more character when they've had a chance to weather a bit. That scarf looks really nice on you, Olive. Brings out your eyes.

Olive Thanks, Hilary. (*She lifts her glass*) Bon appetit.

Hilary Bon appetit.

The telephone rings. Olive consults her watch

That'll be Derek wanting his nightly bulletin.

Olive lifts up the tea cosy and answers the phone

Olive Hello... Fine, thanks, Derek, how's yourself? ... Good. ... Nope, all going according to plan. ... Will you please stop thanking me, Derek. I get really embarrassed the way you keep thanking me. … Certainly. Hold on a second. Would you mind, Hilary?

Hilary hops up and goes to the pyramid, lifts a corner of the cloak

Hilary Sleeping like a baby and still shrinking nicely. (*She drops the cloak*) Tell Derek she's about this length now. (*She describes a length of about twelve inches*)
Olive About twelve inches, Derek.
Hilary I'd say another two days to total de-materialisation. (*She ducks in under the cloak*)
Olive Another two days till she vanishes entirely, Hilary says. … You didn't! Good man yourself! … All right so, Derek. Bye bye for now. (*She hangs up*) Derek sends his best. He's sold another chair, God love him.

Hilary emerges from beneath the blanket, holds up a tiny white towelling bathrobe

Hilary Look at this. Weren't we dopes not to shrink her in the nude. I've always wanted one of those thick towelling bathrobes. It was gorgeous—just like the ones they wear in the films.

The rock begins to tick

Olive Holy Mary! We haven't given poor Orsinara a drop of moisture all day and the poor thing working his little heart out for us!
Hilary Awww. Sorry, Orsinara. Will I give you a wee sup of wine. (*Holding her wine glass, she ducks back under the cloak*)

We hear a hiss of steam. The ticking stops

He's grand now. (*She returns to the table*)

Olive Good. Are you comfy there, Hilary? Wait a tick till I move this over a bit. (*She throws the sheet up and over the table, revealing Monica's suitcases in a pile, largest on top. She moves the cases over a bit, replaces the cloth*) Better?

Hilary Lovely. Thanks very much, Olive.

Olive starts the music. The women pick up their spoons, waiting for the correct phase. When it begins, they click spoons as in Scene 1 and begin to eat. The Lights fade to a single spot, focused on the pyramid. The eating music gives way to the rock's eerie howl. It reaches a peak, stops abruptly and we hear a loud hiccup. The eating music resumes

Fade to black

CURTAIN

FURNITURE AND PROPERTY LIST

Further dressing may be added at the director's discretion.

SCENE 1

On stage: Window curtains
Rug
Small table
Incense sticks
Lighter
Deck of Tarot cards
Picture on the wall, with hand-painted price list on back (described on page 12)
Telephone. *Over it:* tea cosy
Crystals of all shapes and sizes
Mystic images and icons, including angels
Rolled-up futon
Mirror
2 odd-looking chairs
Footstool
Bookshelf. On *it:* stone jar containing money, kitchen timer
Note pad and pen
Wine bottle
Glasses
Cassette player
Folding screen decorated with pictures of angels

Off stage: Pink and purple cushions (**Hilary**)
2 extremely large suitcases, one containing a huge silk scarf (**Ernest**)

Slightly smaller suitcase (**Olive**)
Vanity case containing long emery board (**Monica**)
Two large wooden salad bowls containing wooden spoons
    and food (**Olive** and **Hilary**)
Large oven gloves (**Hilary**)

Personal: **Monica:** handbag containing packet of cigarettes

SCENE 2

Strike: Two large wooden salad bowls

Re-set: Futon
    Various items of clothing from **Monica**'s luggage
    Packet of cigarettes

Off stage: Mug of tea (**Hilary**)
    Carton of yoghurt, small wooden spoon (**Olive**)
    Pile of white pillowcases and a large sack of dried herbs
      (**Hilary**)

Personal: **Bernard:** cap, wallet containing two five pound notes

SCENE 3

Strike: Pillows

Set: White towelling bathrobe

Off stage: 2 long white candles, matches (**Hilary**)
    Eight long poles (**Olive** and **Ernest**)
    Pyramid wrapped in brown paper, tartan shopping bag
      containing smooth dark stone (**Ernest**)

Personal: **Monica:** perfume
    Hilary: shawl

SCENE 4

Re-set: Packet of cigarettes

Personal: **Monica:** lighter

SCENE 5

Set: **Olive**'s big pink cloak
Cassette tape
Tiny white towelling bathrobe

Off stage: Wooden bowls containing wooden spoons and food
(**Hilary**)

Personal: **Olive:** bold costume jewellery, watch
Hilary: bold costume jewellery

LIGHTING PLOT

Property fittings required: nil
1 interior setting

Scene 1

To open: Overall general lighting

Cue 1   **Monica** files her nails to the music   (Page 10)
Slowly fade to black-out

Scene 2

To open: Morning darkness

Cue 2   **Hilary** opens the curtains   (Page 10)
Sunlight through the window

Cue 3   **Olive** and **Hilary** sing a song   (Page 22)
Fade to black-out

Scene 3

To open: Evening lighting

Cue 4   **Hilary** dims the lights   (Page 25)
Fade lighting down

EFFECTS PLOT

Cue 1   **Olive**: "Ahh——"   (Page 2)
            Cheerful horn blast from arriving taxi

Cue 2   **Olive** makes an adjustment to an item on a shelf   (Page 3)
            Loud, impatient doorbell ring

Cue 3   **Monica**: "You're joking, of course."   (Page 5)
            After a little silence, loud clatter of dropped saucepan

Cue 4   **Olive** switches on the cassette player   (Page 9)
            Formless whiny music with an oriental feel;
                cut at end of scene

Cue 5   **Hilary** shakes her head   (Page 12)
            Doorbell rings

Cue 6   **Olive**: "It's all here, clear as crystal."   (Page 15)
            Timer buzzes noisily

Cue 7   **Hilary**: "…guided us to the coal horse."   (Page 17)
            Clippety clop of a horse in the street outside;
                then a whistle, a snort and whinny

Cue 8   **Monica**: "…your legs for years."   (Page 24)
            Doorbell rings

Cue 9   **Olive** puts on a cassette tape   (Page 25)
            Strange, mystical music

Cue 22   Lights fade to a spot   (Page 36)
*Music gives way to the rock's eerie howl,
reaching a peak, stopping abruptly;
loud hiccup; eating music resumes*

www.ingramcontent.com/pod-product-compliance
Ingram Content Group UK Ltd.
Pitfield, Milton Keynes, MK11 3LW, UK
UKHW021822150726
7214IPUK00017B/268